RAW
Chocolate

Matthew Kenney and Meredith Baird

Photographs by Adrian Mueller

GIBBS SMITH
TO ENRICH AND INSPIRE HUMANKIND

First Edition
16 15 14 13 12   5 4 3 2 1

Published by
Gibbs Smith
P.O. Box 667
Layton, Utah 84041

1.800.835.4993 orders
www.gibbs-smith.com

Designed by Drew Furlong
Printed and bound in Hong Kong
Gibbs Smith books are printed on paper produced from sustainable PEFC-certified forest/controlled wood source. Learn more at www.pefc.org.

Library of Congress Cataloging-in-Publication Data

Kenney, Matthew.
  Raw chocolate / Matthew Kenney and Meredith Baird ; photographs by Adrian Mueller. — 1st ed.
      p. cm.
  Includes index.
  ISBN 978-1-4236-2105-8
1. Cooking (Chocolate) 2. Chocolate. 3. Cookbooks. I. Baird, Meredith. II. Title.
  TX767.C5K46 2012
  641.6'374—dc23
                              2011032735

Contents

Acknowledgments

Fiddleheads Artisan Supply, Belfast

Cherished Home, Belfast

The Good Table, Belfast

Chase's Daily, Belfast

Coconut Secrets

Sunfood Nutrition

Left to right: Matthew Kenney, Meredith Baird, Adrian Mueller, and Jessica Acs.

Introduction

What an honor to write about the world's favorite food! So much has been written about chocolate. Chocolate has the ability to define romance, holidays are literally designed around it, and it is hard to imagine a special occasion that doesn't involve the esteemed cacao bean in some form or another. Even those on a diet love "a little chocolate every day." Chocolate does embody the essence of decadence and it's one of those things that we all really seem to enjoy.

Unfortunately, not all chocolate is created equal. Some is truly remarkable—crisp and aromatic, full flavored and nutty—while other chocolate may be sugary, its true origin masked by a grocery list of obscure and often unnecessary ingredients. Much of what we may find in a supermarket today wouldn't even register as chocolate in our minds if it wasn't labeled as such, as it has strayed so far from the exotic and nutritious bean that gives real chocolate its name.

Which brings us to raw chocolate. We wanted to write this book long ago; however, much of the raw chocolate we tried missed the mark, wasn't tempered the way it needed to be, and was often lacking the texture and clarity we expect from fine examples of the product. It just wasn't refined. As with all of the work we do, we aim to develop techniques and flavor combinations that are unique, practical, and inspiring. So here we are, several years and multiple chocolate bars later, finally ready to share what we've found.

With *Raw Chocolate,* we offer our preferred method of preparing and tempering chocolate, as well as a number of other creative uses for cacao products and natural ingredients. These all star in a number of recipes that we hope you'll love as much as we do. We have also tried to standardize working methods that allow you to make these recipes at home regardless of the amount of space you have to work with, and to focus on items that hold up well regardless of the climate you live in.

Chocolate truly embodies the meaning of a daily staple. When friends ask me what I eat when I travel, the answer is simple: chocolate. It also happens to be what I eat after lunch, or when I'm golfing, or in the mood for dessert.

Another reason we have waited until now to write this book is the historical challenge of procuring the best ingredients to make raw chocolate. They are now readily available in gourmet stores or online, as is the equipment needed to produce them.

Perhaps the most exciting aspect of raw chocolate is its contribution to physical and emotional health overall. Cacao, when not cooked, has a tremendously high level of antioxidant properties, and many suggest that it benefits the heart and lowers blood pressure and cholesterol. Who doesn't feel a little—or a lot—better after some great chocolate?

Our Raw Chocolate Philosophy

Preparing artisan chocolate is liberating for a chef in a number of ways. There are fewer ingredients required, and seasonality (something we love to adhere to in general) is not quite as critical. Therefore, the creative inspiration becomes all about technique, redefining taste and texture, and searching for new ways to present a classic.

With chocolate, we have a huge advantage in our overall mission of preparing food that is "sexy," because chocolate already is sexy. In fact, it's hard for it not to be. To us, chocolate making is about inspiring the senses, and literally all of them.

Taste

is always paramount, and its origins are found in high-quality ingredients, something we stress the importance of over and over. Although we love dark chocolate, we're not fans of chocolate that is too bitter. Alternatively, we also would not care for it if the chocolate were too sweet. As with all cooking, balance is everything. We try to embrace flavor profiles that are rooted in classical combinations—we respect cultural inspirations while preparing them in unique and more healthful ways. Chocolate is a great outlet for our inclination to embrace exotic ingredients, such as spices and aromatics. It highlights the fresh, clean flavors that embody all of our work.

Texture

is critical, and without having refined our tempering process, we would not be writing this book. Chocolate bars, bonbons, and other hardened recipes require a snap; chocolate that isn't properly tempered does not feel as good to eat, nor does it look as good in most cases. In many of these recipes, we'll add a sprinkle of sea salt or lavender to the surface of a bar to create another element of texture.

As is so often said, presentation is everything. We believe in investing in attractive molds, wrappers, and other props to always present chocolate in a format that it deserves.

One of the most exciting aspects of raw chocolate is its shelf life. It lasts, and is just as good tomorrow, or the day after that, as it is when freshly made. Always feel free to try a few recipes at once. Things will last—or they may not last, depending on how hungry you are!

Raw Chocolate Handbook

Whereas the preparation of savory raw food requires a lot of thought and planning simply to shop for ingredients, most of the core ingredients for chocolate may be purchased ahead of time and kept on hand. We recommend always keeping cacao paste, beans, butter, nibs, and powder on hand. For sweeteners, we suggest you always have a good quality raw agave, coconut sugar, or another sweetener that you may prefer. Sea salt, high-quality spices, vanilla beans and extract, and other enhancers are always helpful as well. Nuts and seeds are great to have on hand, as long as you store them properly, keeping them cool and dry. If you keep these basics in your pantry, you'll be able to minimize shopping to whatever fresh ingredients your recipe calls for.

Equipment is not terribly complicated with raw chocolate. A good high-quality blender is essential, of course. We prefer Blendtec and use them in our restaurants and at home. You'll also want a high-quality food processor. A dehydrator is needed for the Chocolate Base Recipe and other recipes in this book. One thing that really makes a difference with all food preparation is a set of high-quality, well-sharpened knives; they make life easier and cooking more fun in general. High-quality chocolate molds for both shells and bars are important; they will quickly change the presentation of a recipe for the better. And you'll probably find the need for a couple of extra mixing bowls, pastry bags, an offset spatula, and a good wire whisk when making these recipes. All in all, these are mostly tools that you'll have at home if you work with food on a regular basis.

We strongly recommend, as we do with all of our books, that you fully read the recipes first, and become familiar with the techniques, style, and photographs, in order to take mental notes about what you are making and how. Once you identify your favorite recipes, feel free to experiment, to substitute sweeteners or other components to suit your own taste. One great aspect of chocolate is that, as long as you follow proper tempering technique on the recipes that call for it, the rest is quite forgiving.

Whether your chocolate experience is inspired by taste, hunger, or even romance, you can always take comfort in the fact that it's not only delicious, but nutritious. Enjoy your journey with this amazing bean.

Sweeteners

Just a few short years ago, raw food chefs were thrilled to have access to the latest natural sweetener—the incredibly useful and practical nectar produced from the agave plant. However, numerous opinions have been rendered on the product)some of them wonderful, and others less favorable), many suggesting that all agave is not created equal, may not be 100 percent raw, or that it is not as healthy as other sweeteners. Although our opinion is that some of the commentary is overblown on both sides of the argument, we would like to offer you options in addition to agave for your chocolate-making experience.

Coconut Nectar

Coconut nectar, like agave, is a very low glycemic liquid sweetener derived from the liquid sap of coconut blossoms. It naturally contains many minerals and vitamins, including broad spectrum Bs and vitamin C. To create the nectar, the sap is evaporated at allegedly low temperatures. Although it is certainly much less processed than most commercial sweeteners, it is still a processed sweetener. The flavor is mild, but the color and flavor is slightly richer than agave, which makes it an excellent partner to dark chocolate.

Palm Sugar

Palm sugar is the only nonliquid sweetener we recommend in these recipes. Because of its low melting temperature, it is suitable to substitute for a liquid sweetener. Palm sugar is minimally processed and sustainable, but it is generally not considered a raw product. Palm sugar is low on the glycemic index and full of a broad spectrum of vitamins and minerals similar to those found in coconut nectar. It has a very neutral, but deep flavor that makes it an excellent sweetener for chocolate.

Maple Syrup

All maple syrups are not created equal. Commercial maple syrup is highly processed and often contains food coloring. In the United States, if the product on the shelf is in fact labeled "Maple Syrup," it must come from the maple tree. Real maple syrup is produced by heating the mildly sweet sap over boiling water to evaporate and concentrate the sugars. Maple syrup is not considered to be a raw product, nor is it low on the glycemic index, but it is very high in manganese and zinc, which is beneficial in energy production, and immune and antioxidant defense. Compared to other sweeteners, maple syrup is a relatively local product, especially if you live in the Northeastern United States. Maple syrup has its characteristic "maple" flavor, which we find delicious.

Honey

Honey is perhaps the only truly raw sweetener on the market, as it is produced, harvested, and left in its natural state to consume. Like most products on the market, commercial honey does not fit the healthy bill because it is processed and reduced to a state that is a far cry from natural. We recommend raw, preferably local, honey. Honey has a wide variety of health benefits and is perhaps the most healing of all sweeteners on the market. Honey is antibacterial and antimicrobial, which makes it a great sweetener to use in the case of many ailments. However, honey is not vegan, so for people wishing to eschew all animal products from their diet, honey may not be an option. Honey has a very distinct and powerful flavor, especially in its raw state, so it may not be the best substitute in chocolate. Although, if you are a honey lovers like we are, go for it!

The thing to remember is that desserts, especially chocolate desserts, are decadent and a luxury. While we do subscribe to the philosophy that daily chocolate consumption is good for health and wellness, we also prescribe moderation. Any sweetener should be consumed within reason. Both from personal experience and research, we do still currently advocate agave as a sweetener of choice for chocolate. At the same time, we understand that opinions and tastes can vary, and we always try to encourage experimentation and adjustment of our recipes. Feel free to try the many options and do what feels, and tastes, best for you.

Chocolate Base Recipe

2½ cups cacao liquor (paste)*
2 cups cacao butter**
1 tablespoon vanilla extract
½ cup liquid sweetener
Salt

Finely chop cacao paste and cacao butter. Place in a metal bowl. Dehydrate at 115 degrees F for approximately 1 hour until two-thirds of the chocolate is melted. Stir occasionally to increase the speed of the melting process. Once two-thirds is melted, remove bowl from dehydrator and stir until all chocolate is completely melted. Add vanilla, liquid sweetener, and salt. Continue to stir until well combined. (If mixture starts to thicken, place immediately back in the dehydrator.) Once all ingredients are combined, place back in the dehydrator and warm mixture for approximately 5 minutes. You don't want the chocolate to exceed 88 degrees F at this point. Remove from dehydrator. Your chocolate should now be tempered and ready to pour into molds. In order to test if your chocolate is tempered, pour a drop on wax paper and allow it to cool. If it becomes firm and shiny then it is properly and correctly tempered.

To properly make chocolate, it is essential that every utensil you use be very dry. Moisture will cause the chocolate to seize, which means the oil will separate from the other ingredients. If this does happen you can blend the chocolate with a touch of warm water in a high-speed blender to bring it back together. Although the chocolate is not ruined if this happens, it will no longer be possible to properly temper it, so it must be stored in the refrigerator in order to stay firm.

* Substitute 2½ cups cacao oil for a white chocolate base.

** Substitute 2 cups sifted coconut flour for a white chocolate base.

Makes enough for approximately 1 dozen chocolate bars

Chocolate Shells
Recipe

1 mold of your choice

**1 melted, tempered batch of Chocolate Base
(page 11)**

Making the bonbon shells

Lay room-temperature molds on a flat surface.

Completely fill each mold with tempered chocolate. Scrape excess chocolate from the mold with an offset spatula. You want the edges of each mold to be clean. Gently tap the mold on the counter until you remove all of the air bubbles.

Turn the filled mold upside down over a large empty bowl, pouring out the majority of the chocolate and leaving only enough chocolate to coat the entire opening of each mold.

Set the coated mold in the refrigerator for approximately 10 minutes to firm. You don't want it to set too long or it will crack when it is brought back to room temperature.

Remove from the refrigerator. Your chocolate "shells" are now ready to fill.

Makes enough for approximately 2 dozen chocolate shells

Filling the bonbon shells

When filling chocolate shells, make sure that each filling is room temperature. The filling should be malleable (or liquid) enough to fill the mold. The amount of filling that you use depends somewhat on the style and size of mold, but the standard amount of filling is approximately 1 tablespoon per chocolate.

For fillings that have a more liquid consistency, it is easiest to use a polypropylene pastry bag with a very small opening.

For fillings that have a dough-like consistency, you can roll them into a ball and place in the center of the bonbon shell.

Fill the chocolate shells in the mold to approximately ⅛ inch from the top with the filling of your choice.

Once chocolate molds are filled, return to the refrigerator for 5 minutes so that the filling can set.

Remove filled chocolate from refrigerator. Using a spoon, cover the filling with prepared chocolate to the top of the mold.

Tap the mold on the counter to remove all air bubbles and to level the chocolate.

Scrape excess chocolate from the mold with an offset spatula.

Return filled chocolate to the refrigerator and allow to set for at least one hour before you try to remove the chocolate from the molds.

When chocolate is ready, it should release easily from the mold when the mold is turned upside down and gently tapped.

Masculine

The flavors of our chocolate bars are simple and elegant with nuances that resemble the finest perfume. These flavors are intended to be delicate and subtle. Over time, we realized that our chocolate bars were taking on aromatic influences that leaned toward either the masculine or feminine. These are our masculine-influenced bars. Think of them as our Grey Flannel line.

Extreme Dark

Chocolate in its essence: dark, smoky, and powerful.

**1 melted, tempered batch of Chocolate Base
(page 11)**

Pour chocolate into a bar mold in the style of your choice. Place in the refrigerator to firm.

Makes approximately 1 dozen bars

Lavender, Gray Salt

Our base has salt, although in certain instances, additional salt is part of the actual flavor of a recipe. In this case, along with the lavender, the salt creates a bar that, while still sweet, also has a bit of savory personality.

1 melted, tempered batch of Chocolate Base (page 11)

2 tablespoons dried lavender

1 tablespoon gray salt

Pour chocolate into a bar mold in the style of your choice. Before chocolate is solid, sprinkle with lavender and salt. Place in the refrigerator to firm.

Makes approximately 1 dozen bars

Saffron

Saffron is such a beautiful and wondrous spice. However, it must be very fresh. It will be well worth your effort to source it so that you can be assured of its freshness and quality.

1 melted, tempered batch of Chocolate Base (page 11)

1 teaspoon saffron threads

While the chocolate is melting and tempering, add the saffron threads. You want to make sure to add them while the chocolate is warm in order to release the flavor. Pour chocolate into a bar mold in the style of your choice. Place in the refrigerator to firm.

Makes approximately 1 dozen bars

Anise

Most Mediterranean countries have unique varieties of anise liqueurs. For something sweet, try the Italian sambuca. If you prefer the anise flavor to be really intense, make this recipe with the Turkish Raki.

2 tablespoons ground anise

1 tablespoon anise-flavored liqueur, such as pastis (optional)

1 melted, tempered batch of Chocolate Base (page 11)

Stir ground anise and liqueur into melted, tempered chocolate before firming. Pour chocolate into a bar mold in the style of your choice. Place in the refrigerator to firm.

Makes approximately 1 dozen bars

Mint and Candied Nib

If you're making one chocolate for Father's Day, this would be it. (Your mother will love it, too.)

1 tablespoon peppermint extract

1 tablespoon coconut sugar, powdered in a
    spice grinder

2 tablespoons cacao nibs

1 melted, tempered batch of Chocolate Base
    (page 11)

Garnish

2 tablespoons cacao nibs

Stir peppermint extract, coconut sugar, and cacao nibs into tempered chocolate before firming. Pour chocolate into a bar mold in the style of your choice. Garnish back with cacao nibs. Place in the refrigerator to firm.

Makes approximately 1 dozen bars

Salt and Pepper

Here is a good opportunity for you to be creative, simply by using any variety of salts, such as Himalayan Pink, or Black Lava, and even different peppercorns, such as red, white, or other varieties.

1 melted, tempered batch of Chocolate Base (page 11)

2 tablespoons high-quality rock salt

1 tablespoon freshly ground peppercorns

Pour chocolate into a bar mold in the style of your choice. Sprinkle the back with salt and pepper. Place in the refrigerator to firm.

Makes approximately 1 dozen bars

Basil

Whereas we typically prefer to work with fresh herbs, the pungency of the dried basil was a better fit for the coconut sugar in this recipe.

2 tablespoons dried basil, finely powdered in a spice grinder

2 tablespoons coconut sugar, finely powdered in a spice grinder

1 melted, tempered batch of Chocolate Base (page 11)

1 tablespoon fresh baby basil leaves (optional)

Stir dried basil and coconut sugar into melted, tempered chocolate before firming. Pour chocolate into a bar mold in the style of your choice. Sprinkle the back with fresh baby basil if using. Place in the refrigerator to firm.

Makes approximately 1 dozen bars

Rosemary

Rosemary, deriving from the Latin phrase, "dew of the sea," is pungent and aromatic. Most people love this flavor; however, it can be quite overpowering, so use in moderation.

2 tablespoons dried rosemary, powdered
   in a spice grinder

1 tablespoon coconut sugar, powdered
   in a spice grinder

1 melted, tempered batch of Chocolate Base
   (page 11)

Garnish

1 tablespoon dried rosemary

Stir rosemary and coconut sugar into tempered chocolate before firming. Pour chocolate into a bar mold in the style of your choice. Garnish back with dried rosemary. Place in the refrigerator to firm.

Makes approximately 1 dozen bars

Juniper

The juniper berry is famous for its presence in gin. Although just as intoxicating in a chocolate bar, you'll have no problem driving when eating this!

2 tablespoons juniper berries, crushed

1 tablespoon juniper Schnapps, such as Doornkaat (optional)

1 melted, tempered batch of Chocolate Base (page 11)

Stir juniper berries and schnapps, if using, into tempered chocolate before firming. Pour chocolate into a bar mold in the style of your choice. Place in the refrigerator to firm.

Makes approximately 1 dozen bars

Chia Crunch

Good chocolate is not just about taste—it is equally important to achieve texture that creates variation and a fulfilling experience. The chia is a great addition to this already crisp dark bar.

3 tablespoons chia seeds

1 tablespoon coconut sugar, powdered in a spice grinder

1 melted, tempered batch of Chocolate Base (page 11)

Stir chia seeds and coconut sugar into tempered chocolate before firming. Pour chocolate into a bar mold in the style of your choice. Place in the refrigerator to firm.

Makes approximately 1 dozen bars

Feminine

These are some of our most exotic, yet simple recipes. Just as chocolate is robust and powerful enough to carry the intense flavors of our masculine chapter, it is also elegant and subtle in a way that lends itself to the more refined ingredients we've included in this chapter. Men need not shy away from these recipes, despite their gender reference!

Asian Sesame

Sesame oil is known as the "queen of oils," for its nourishing benefits to our bodies and its antioxidant properties. It also happens to be delicious with chocolate.

2 tablespoons sesame oil

1 melted, tempered batch of Chocolate Base
(page 11)

Garnish
2 tablespoons sesame seeds

Stir sesame oil into melted, tempered chocolate before firming. Pour chocolate into a bar mold in the style of your choice. Garnish the top with sesame seeds. Place in the refrigerator to firm.

Makes approximately 1 dozen bars

Rose and Pink Salt

Himalayan crystal salt is quite readily available in health and specialty shops these days. I prefer a salt that is a bit coarse, so it adds texture and also a bit more flavor. This is a great dish for a holiday (hint: Valentine's Day).

2 tablespoons rose water

1 teaspoon Himalayan salt

1 melted, tempered batch of Chocolate Base
(page 11)

Garnish

2 tablespoons dried rose petals, crushed*

½ tablespoon high-quality Himalayan rock salt

Stir rose water and salt into melted, tempered chocolate before firming. Pour chocolate into a bar mold in the style of your choice. Garnish the back with dried rose petals and rock salt. Place in the refrigerator to firm.

* You can find dried rose petals in the bulk tea section of your health food store.

Makes approximately 1 dozen bars

Vanilla Bean (White Chocolate)

We often hear of "milk and honey" to describe simple, elegant comfort, although "vanilla and chocolate" should surely be nominated. The better the quality and freshness of the vanilla beans, the more you'll love this simple bar.

2 vanilla beans, scraped

1 melted, tempered batch of White Chocolate Base (page 11)

Stir vanilla into tempered chocolate before firming. Pour chocolate into a bar mold in the style of your choice. Place in the refrigerator to firm.

Makes approximately 1 dozen bars

Elderflower

In addition to its aromatic and gentle flavor, elder-flower is said to have considerable antiviral properties, as well as the ability to contribute to a healthy immune system.

2 tablespoons dried elderflower, ground
   in a spice grinder

2 tablespoons elderflower liqueur, such as
   St. Germain (optional)

1 melted, tempered batch of Chocolate Base
   (page 11)

Garnish

1 tablespoon dried elderflower

Stir dried elderflower and elderflower liqueur, if using, into tempered chocolate before firming. Pour chocolate into a bar mold in the style of your choice. Garnish the back with dried elderflower. Place in the refrigerator to firm.

Makes approximately 1 dozen bars

Citrus Honeysuckle

If certain wines or teas are made for sipping, this chocolate is made for nibbling. It's one of those summer afternoon bars that you keep around and savor, a little at a time.

2 tablespoons honey

1 teaspoon dried honeysuckle tea flowers*

2 tablespoons lemon zest

1 melted, tempered batch of Chocolate Base
  (page 11)

Garnish

1 tablespoon dried honeysuckle tea flowers,
  crushed

1 tablespoon lemon zest

Stir honey, honeysuckle flowers, and lemon zest into tempered chocolate before firming. Pour chocolate into a bar mold in the style of your choice. Garnish the back with honeysuckle flowers and lemon zest. Place in the refrigerator to firm.

* You can find dried honeysuckle tea flowers in the bulk tea section of your health food store.

Makes approximately 1 dozen bars

Nutmeg

When using nutmeg, it is always preferable to grind it fresh, just before using it. The flavor difference will be remarkable and well worth the few seconds of extra effort.

1 melted, tempered batch of Chocolate Base (page 11)

2 teaspoons freshly ground nutmeg

Stir nutmeg into tempered chocolate before firming. Pour chocolate into a bar mold in the style of your choice. Place in the refrigerator to firm.

Makes approximately 1 dozen bars

Candied Nasturtium

Nasturtiums are the most well-known edible flower, and favored for their peppery, sweet essence.

1 cup fresh nasturtium flowers

¼ cup coconut sugar, powdered in a spice grinder

1 melted, tempered batch of Chocolate Base (page 11)

Dry the nasturtium flowers in a dehydrator for at least 12 hours and powder in a spice grinder to create a dust. Combine nasturtium dust and coconut sugar. Reserve a few tablespoons for garnish.

Stir nasturtium and coconut sugar into tempered chocolate before firming. Pour chocolate into a bar mold in the style of your choice. Sprinkle the back with reserved nasturtium dust. Place in the refrigerator to firm.

Makes approximately 1 dozen bars

Hazelnut Almond

Imagine a Mon Chéri with a little added almond for flavor, and here you are.

¼ cup hazelnuts, finely chopped

¼ cup almonds, finely chopped

1 teaspoon almond extract

1 melted, tempered batch of Chocolate Base (page 11)

Garnish

¼ cup hazelnuts, chopped

¼ cup almonds, chopped

1 tablespoon coarse Himalayan salt

Stir hazelnuts, almonds, and almond extract into tempered chocolate before firming. Pour chocolate into a bar mold in the style of your choice. Sprinkle the back with remaining chopped hazelnuts, almonds, and salt. Place in the refrigerator to firm.

Makes approximately 1 dozen bars

Intense Orange

This simple technique of candied orange can be used to flavor a variety of raw chocolates—from truffles to bars to bonbons.

1 melted, tempered batch of Chocolate Base (page 11)

2 tablespoons orange zest

Garnish

¼ cup long, thin strips of orange peel

1 tablespoon liquid sweetener

To make the candied orange garnish, toss orange peel with liquid sweetener and dehydrate for approximately 24 hours.

To make bars, stir orange zest into tempered chocolate before firming. Pour chocolate into a bar mold in the style of your choice. Garnish the back with candied orange peels. Place in the refrigerator to firm.

Makes approximately 1 dozen bars

Honey Thyme

With so many varieties of raw honey available these days, and depending on your taste preferences, you may end up with many different results when using honey with chocolate. For the thyme to come through, it is best to use a honey that is mild. Alternatively, a strong honey, like manuka, may be interesting on its own without the herb.

2 tablespoons raw honey

2 tablespoons dried thyme

1 melted, tempered batch of Chocolate Base (page 11)

Stir honey and thyme into tempered chocolate before firming. Pour chocolate into a bar mold in the style of your choice. Place in the refrigerator to firm.

Makes approximately 1 dozen bars

Truffles

Just to show how far raw has come, Wikipedia now lists an additional truffle category along with the American, European, and Swiss versions: the Raw Truffle. Truffles, named after their delectable fungus counterpart, are small, often round or roundish knobs of richness, and are the ideal vehicle to showcase the abundance of impressive raw ingredients now available. They're truly easy to create and offer a lot of forgiveness when adding additional flavors or making adjustments, so have fun and experiment!

Triple M: Maca, Mesquite, Maqui

All our favorite superfoods in one bite! Maqui is a recently available purple powder, rich in antioxidants, with a unique tartness that balances the sweet.

1 cup cacao powder

¾ cup liquid sweetener

1 tablespoon maca powder

½ tablespoon mesquite powder

1 teaspoon maqui powder

1 teaspoon vanilla extract

½ teaspoon salt

1 cup cacao butter, liquefied

½ cup coconut oil

Garnish

2 tablespoons maca powder

2 tablespoons mesquite powder

2 tablespoons maqui powder

Sift powders together for garnish and set aside.

Blend all ingredients except for the cacao butter and coconut oil in a high-powered blender until smooth. Slowly add the cacao butter and coconut oil. Continue to blend until completely incorporated. Pour into a bowl and place in the refrigerator for 15 to 30 minutes until mixture becomes firm enough to scoop and mold. Using a small ice cream scoop, form mixture into small balls, about 2 tablespoons each. Roll in sifted powders to coat.

Makes approximately 2 dozen truffles

Meyer Lemon, Goji

Truffles are great little packets of surprise, and given that they don't require large amounts of any one ingredient, they're ideal for incorporating exotic flavors. Meyer lemon and goji are a couple of ideas, but also consider saffron, lemon grass, kaffir lime . . . there are endless options.

1¼ cups cashews, soaked

1 cup liquid sweetener

1 tablespoon vanilla extract

1 vanilla bean, scraped

3 tablespoons Meyer lemon zest

½ teaspoon salt

1 cup cacao butter, liquefied

½ cup coconut oil

½ cup coconut butter

½ cup goji berries, finely chopped

Garnish

Coconut sugar powdered in a spice grinder

Blend the first six ingredients in a high-powered blender until smooth. Slowly add the cacao butter, coconut oil, and coconut butter. Continue to blend until completely incorporated. Stir in the goji berries. Pour into a bowl and place in the refrigerator for 15 to 30 minutes until mixture becomes firm enough to scoop and mold. Using a small ice cream scoop, form mixture into small balls, about 2 tablespoons each. Roll in powdered coconut sugar to garnish.

Makes approximately 2 dozen truffles

Matcha Tea

This is our simplest and most elegant truffle. While we often suggest options to adjust recipes, this one has fully evolved and stands as is.

1 cup cacao powder

¾ cup liquid sweetener

2 tablespoons matcha tea powder

1 teaspoon vanilla extract

½ teaspoon salt

1 cup cacao butter, liquefied

½ cup coconut oil

Garnish
¼ cup matcha tea powder

Blend all ingredients except for the cacao butter and coconut oil in a high-powered blender until smooth. Slowly add the cacao butter and coconut oil. Continue to blend until completely incorporated. Pour into a bowl and place in the refrigerator for 15 to 30 minutes until mixture becomes firm enough to scoop and mold. Using a small ice cream scoop, form mixture into small balls, about 2 tablespoons each. Roll in matcha tea powder to coat.

Makes approximately 2 dozen truffles

Rocher

Although *rocher* means "rock" in French, the product is actually made in Italy by the same geniuses who produce Nutella. This textural wonder in our raw chocolate truffle is also related in flavor to gianduja, or hazelnut-flavored chocolate.

1¼ cups cacao powder

1 cup liquid sweetener

1 teaspoon vanilla extract

1 teaspoon hazelnut extract

½ teaspoon salt

1 cup cacao butter, liquefied

½ cup coconut oil

½ cup hazelnuts, chopped (reserve ¼ cup for garnish)

¼ cup coconut sugar, powdered in a spice grinder

Blend the first five ingredients in a high-powered blender until smooth. Slowly add the cacao butter and coconut oil. Continue to blend until completely incorporated. Stir in chopped hazelnuts and coconut sugar. Pour into a bowl and place in the refrigerator for 15 to 30 minutes until mixture becomes firm enough to scoop and mold. Using a small ice cream scoop, form mixture into small balls, about 2 tablespoons each. Roll in remaining chopped hazelnuts to garnish.

Makes approximately 2 dozen truffles

Milk Chocolate

Of course, any nut milk would be a fine substitute for almond and the flavor of the truffle will change accordingly. Pistachio is one great alternative.

1½ cups cacao powder

¾ cup liquid sweetener

¼ cup almond milk

1 teaspoon vanilla extract

1 vanilla bean, scraped

½ teaspoon salt

1 cup cacao butter, liquefied

½ cup coconut oil

¼ cup coconut butter

Garnish
¼ cup sifted cacao powder

Blend all ingredients except for the cacao butter, coconut oil, and coconut butter in a high-powered blender until smooth. Slowly add the cacao butter, coconut oil, and coconut butter. Continue to blend until completely incorporated. Pour into a bowl and place in the refrigerator for 15 to 30 minutes until mixture becomes firm enough to scoop and mold. Using a small ice cream scoop, form mixture into small balls, about 2 tablespoons each. Roll in cacao powder to coat.

Makes approximately 2 dozen truffles

Sweet Almond

Extracts are ideal for flavoring chocolate and pastries—in this case, use sweet almond. As you'll see in our other recipes, we also love aromatics such as peppermint.

1¼ cups cacao powder

1 cup liquid sweetener

1 teaspoon vanilla extract

1 teaspoon almond extract

½ teaspoon salt

1 cup cacao butter, liquefied

½ cup coconut oil

½ cup almonds, chopped (reserve ¼ cup for garnish)

Blend all ingredients except for the cacao butter, coconut oil, and almonds in a high-powered blender until smooth. Slowly add the cacao butter and coconut oil. Continue to blend until completely incorporated. Stir in chopped almonds. Pour into a bowl and place in the refrigerator for 15 to 30 minutes until mixture becomes firm enough to scoop and mold. Using a small ice cream scoop, form mixture into small balls, about 2 tablespoons each. Roll in remaining chopped almonds to garnish.

Makes approximately 2 dozen truffles

Black Sesame

Consider this a raw halvah truffle. Although we have minimized the use of honey in this book, it is a great substitute for agave in this case and enhances the Mediterranean nature of the dish.

1¼ cups cacao powder

1 cup agave or honey

1 teaspoon vanilla extract

1 tablespoon sesame oil

¼ cup tahini

½ teaspoon salt

1 cup cacao butter, liquefied

½ cup coconut oil

Garnish

¼ cup black sesame seeds

Blend all ingredients except for the cacao butter and coconut oil in a high-powered blender until smooth. Slowly add the cacao butter and coconut oil. Continue to blend until completely incorporated. Pour into a bowl and place in the refrigerator for 15 to 30 minutes until mixture becomes firm enough to scoop and mold. Using a small ice cream scoop, form mixture into small balls, about 2 tablespoons each. Roll in sesame seeds to garnish.

Makes approximately 2 dozen truffles

Toasted Coconut

A quick hint about coconut oil: although we only use extra virgin and raw coconut oil and butter, some have more of that "coconut flavor" than others. For a dish that emphasizes coconut, a strong coconut oil is ideal, but we always try to keep a couple of different types of coconut oil on hand and take this into consideration when making a dish so you don't get an overpowering coconut flavor unless you want to.

1¼ cups cashews, soaked

1 cup liquid sweetener

1 tablespoon vanilla extract

1 vanilla bean, scraped

½ teaspoon salt

1 cup cacao butter, liquefied

½ cup coconut oil

½ cup coconut butter

Garnish
¼ cup coconut flakes powdered in a spice
    grinder

Blend all ingredients except for the cacao butter, coconut oil, and coconut butter in a high-powered blender until smooth. Slowly add the cacao butter, coconut oil, and coconut butter. Continue to blend until completely incorporated. Pour into a bowl and place in the refrigerator for 15 to 30 minutes until mixture becomes firm enough to scoop and mold. Using a small ice cream scoop, form mixture into small balls, about 2 tablespoons each. Roll in powdered coconut to garnish.

Makes approximately 2 dozen truffles

Midnight Mint

As with the Rocher and others, we're going for texture here, as well as the cool mint flavor, which lightens the richness of the recipe.

1¼ cups cacao powder

¾ cup liquid sweetener

1 teaspoon vanilla extract

2 teaspoons peppermint extract

½ teaspoon salt

1 cup cacao butter, liquefied

½ cup coconut oil

Garnish

¼ cup cacao nibs

Blend all ingredients except for the cacao butter and coconut oil in a high-powered blender until smooth. Slowly add the cacao butter and coconut oil. Continue to blend until completely incorporated. Pour into a bowl and place in the refrigerator for 15 to 30 minutes until mixture becomes firm enough to scoop and mold. Using a small ice cream scoop, form mixture into small balls, about 2 tablespoons each. Roll in cacao nibs to garnish.

Makes approximately 2 dozen truffles

Maple Pecan

This is our nod to the Northeast. It's a flavor that could also be a summer ice cream, with all the elements of butterscotch.

1¼ cups cacao powder

¾ cup maple syrup

1 teaspoon vanilla extract

1 vanilla bean, scraped

½ teaspoon salt

1 cup cacao butter, liquefied

½ cup coconut oil

Garnish

¼ cup pecans powdered in a high-powered blender or spice grinder

Blend all ingredients except for the cacao butter and coconut oil in a high-powered blender until smooth. Slowly add the cacao butter and coconut oil. Continue to blend until completely incorporated. Pour into a bowl and place in the refrigerator for 15 to 30 minutes until mixture becomes firm enough to scoop and mold. Using a small ice cream scoop, form mixture into small balls, about 2 tablespoons each. Roll in pecan powder to garnish.

Makes approximately 2 dozen truffles

Bonbons

Sometimes, modesty is the most challenging thing to live up to. Bonbons, a modest chocolate simply named as something "good," are certainly that and more when well prepared. Yet there is also an elegance associated with them that gives us pause, applies a little pressure in the way we think about constructing them, and always keeps us on our toes in fear of not living up to the delicious history they embody. Our bonbons are a bit more work than truffles, yet they are more stable, sophisticated, and genuinely good.

Pistachio Nougat

I've always been fascinated by exotic Mediterranean flavors, and the luxurious, aromatic sweetness that often represents them. Pistachio and rose water seem like a marriage of Morocco and Sicily.

Approximately 2 dozen molded chocolate shells (page 12)

Filling

½ cup cashews

½ cup macadamia nuts

¾ cup liquid sweetener

¼ cup honey

3 tablespoons almond extract

1 tablespoon rose water

1 tablespoon vanilla extract

Pinch sea salt

¾ cup coconut oil, melted

1½ cups coconut flour

1 cup pistachios

Filling
Blend all ingredients except coconut flour and pistachios until smooth. In a food processor, combine coconut flour and the blended mixture. Mix well until smooth. Place mixture in the refrigerator until it begins to harden but is still malleable. Once the mixture is slightly firm, fold in pistachios. This is a relatively firm filling. Roll into balls according to the size of your mold in order to fill chocolate shells.

Assembly
Follow directions on page 13 to fill shells.

Makes approximately 2 dozen chocolates

Honey Chamomile

A tip to remember when creating chocolate recipes: flavors that work well in tea and coffee drinks are, in general, equally successful when paired with chocolate.

Approximately 2 dozen molded chocolate shells (page 12)

Filling

1 cup honey

¼ cup brewed chamomile tea

1 tablespoon vanilla extract

Pinch sea salt

¾ cup coconut oil, melted

Filling

Blend all ingredients until smooth. In order to fill chocolate molds, you will want to place mixture in a pastry bag with a very thin tip.

Assembly

Follow directions on page 13 to fill shells.

Makes approximately 2 dozen chocolates

Lemon Basil

Should you be fortunate enough to live in an area where fresh lemon basil is available locally, we highly recommend you use it in place of traditional basil when it is in season.

Approximately 2 dozen molded chocolate shells (page 12)

Filling

½ cup cashews

½ cup macadamia nuts

¾ cup liquid sweetener

¼ cup lemon juice

2 tablespoons minced fresh basil or lemon basil

1 tablespoon lemon zest

1 tablespoon vanilla extract

Pinch sea salt

¾ cup coconut oil, melted

1½ cups coconut flour

Filling

Blend all ingredients except coconut flour until smooth. In a food processor, combine the coconut flour and the blended mixture. Mix well until smooth. Place mixture in the refrigerator until it begins to harden, but is still malleable. This is a relatively firm filling. Roll into balls according to the size of your mold in order to fill chocolate shells.

Assembly

Follow directions on page 13 to fill shells.

Makes approximately 2 dozen chocolates

Almond Buttercup

You may wish to consider any number of variations on the almond buttercup. Substitute other nuts or sweeteners, or even add essential oils, citrus zest, or spices.

Approximately 2 dozen molded chocolate shells (page 12)

Filling

1½ cups almond butter

¾ cup liquid sweetener

¼ cup honey

2 tablespoons coconut sugar, powdered in a spice grinder

1 tablespoon vanilla extract

1 tablespoon sea salt

Filling
Blend all ingredients until smooth. This mixture has a medium-thick consistency. In order to fill chocolate molds, you will want to place mixture in a pastry bag with a ¼-inch tip.

Assembly
Follow directions on page 13 to fill shells.

Makes approximately 2 dozen chocolates

Peppermint Crème

You'll notice the spirulina as an optional addition to this recipe. It's a quirky addition to mint chocolate. Along with some added nutrition, it also gives a nice minty color, naturally.

Approximately 2 dozen molded chocolate shells (page 12)

Filling

½ cup cashews

½ cup macadamia nuts

¾ cup liquid sweetener

¼ cup honey

3 tablespoons peppermint extract

1 tablespoon vanilla extract

Pinch sea salt

1 tablespoon spirulina (optional)

¾ cup coconut oil, melted

1½ cups coconut flour

Filling
Blend all ingredients except coconut flour until smooth. In a food processor, combine coconut flour and the blended mixture. Mix well until smooth. Place mixture in the refrigerator until it begins to harden, but is still malleable. This is a relatively firm filling. Roll into balls according to the size of your mold in order to fill chocolate shells.

Assembly
Follow directions on page 13 to fill shells.

Makes approximately 2 dozen chocolates

Marzipan

Although traditional marzipan is prepared with almonds, they are blanched and peeled. Raw almonds, with their skins, do not offer the same luxurious texture, which is the reason we use cashews and macadamias in this recipe.

Approximately 2 dozen molded chocolate shells (page 12)

Filling

½ cup cashews

½ cup macadamia nuts

1 cup liquid sweetener

3 tablespoons almond extract

1 tablespoon vanilla extract

Pinch sea salt

¾ cup coconut oil, melted

1½ cups coconut flour

Filling

Blend all ingredients except coconut flour until smooth. In a food processor, combine the coconut flour and the blended mixture. Mix well until smooth. Place mixture in the refrigerator until it begins to harden, but is still malleable. This is a relatively firm filling. Roll into balls according to the size of your mold in order to fill chocolate shells.

Assembly

Follow directions on page 13 to fill shells.

Makes approximately 2 dozen chocolates

Dark Chocolate

This is a basic go-to bonbon. It's also a great foundation for adding additional flavors, such as candied orange, lemon zest, honeycomb, or whatever suits your taste.

Approximately 2 dozen molded chocolate shells (page 12)

Filling

1 cup cacao powder

1 cup liquid sweetener

1 vanilla bean, scraped

Pinch sea salt

1 cup coconut oil, melted

½ cup cacao oil, melted

½ cup coconut butter, liquefied

Filling

Blend all ingredients until smooth. Place mixture in the refrigerator until it begins to harden, but is still malleable. This is a relatively firm filling. It should have a fudge-like consistency. Roll into balls according to the size of your mold in order to fill chocolate shells.

Assembly

Follow directions on page 13 to fill shells.

Makes approximately 2 dozen chocolates

Mesquite, Maple, Walnut

Just as color variation works well in a painting, contrasting flavors work well in a recipe. We quite often pair contrasting ingredients of a similar texture—in this case woodsy and earthy. It creates a more subtle, yet interesting, flavor profile.

Approximately 2 dozen molded chocolate shells (page 12)

Filling

1 cup walnut butter

½ cup coconut oil, melted

1 cup maple syrup

2 tablespoons mesquite powder

1 tablespoon vanilla extract

1 tablespoon sea salt

½ cup walnuts, chopped

Filling

Blend all ingredients except walnuts until smooth. Place mixture in the refrigerator until it begins to harden, but is still malleable. Once the mixture is slightly firm, fold in walnuts. This is a relatively firm filling. Roll into balls according to the size of your mold in order to fill chocolate shells.

Assembly

Follow directions on page 13 to fill shells.

Makes approximately 2 dozen chocolates

Chocolate Chai

One of our more exotic chocolates, this is excellent with a cup of almond milk.

Approximately 2 dozen molded chocolate shells (page 12)

Filling

1 cup cashews

½ cup cacao powder

1 cup liquid sweetener

1 tablespoon vanilla extract

1 tablespoon cinnamon

1 teaspoon nutmeg

1 teaspoon ginger

1 vanilla bean, scraped

Pinch sea salt

¾ cup coconut oil, melted

Filling

Blend all ingredients except coconut oil until smooth. Blend in coconut oil last, and mix well until smooth. Place mixture in the refrigerator until it begins to harden, but is still malleable. This is a relatively firm filling. It should have a fudge-like consistency. Roll into balls according to the size of your mold in order to fill chocolate shells.

Assembly

Follow directions on page 13 to fill shells.

Makes approximately 2 dozen chocolates`

Salted Caramel

The combination of caramel and chocolate is classic, but when you add a touch of salt it becomes divine. To us, this might be the most perfect combination.

Approximately 2 dozen molded chocolate shells (page 12)

Filling

1 cup macadamia nuts

½ cup cashews

1 cup liquid sweetener

1 tablespoon vanilla extract

½ teaspoon sea salt

¾ cup coconut oil, melted

Filling

Blend all ingredients except coconut oil until smooth. In a food processor, combine the coconut oil and the blended mixture. Mix well until smooth. Place mixture in the refrigerator until it begins to harden, but is still malleable. This is a relatively firm filling. Roll into balls according to the size of your mold in order to fill chocolate shells.

Assembly

Follow directions on page 13 to fill shells.

Makes approximately 2 dozen chocolates

Fudge

Southern in spirit only, our fudge is all about elegance. While its roots may be found in our childhood favorites, the ingredients we use to create the fudge-like texture and density are as natural as can be. While some chocolate recipes are a bit more challenging, these are among the easiest—great for a beginner and universally appealing.

White Chocolate Fudge

Possibly the distant healthy relative of childhood-favorite divinity, this white chocolate fudge is indeed divine, with a lot less sugar.

1 cup cashews, soaked

1 cup cacao butter, liquefied

½ cup coconut butter

1 cup liquid sweetener

2 tablespoons vanilla extract

4 tablespoons water

Pinch salt

Blend all ingredients until smooth.

Prepare a 9-inch square cheesecake pan by greasing the sides with coconut oil and lining the bottom with parchment paper. Pour blended ingredients into prepared pan. Freeze for at least 1 hour to set. Fudge can be stored in the freezer or refrigerator for several weeks.

Makes approximately 3 dozen 1-inch pieces

Milk Chocolate Chai

Chai, most common in aromatic Indian teas, also balances other earthy flavors, chocolate being an ideal outlet for it. Due to its intensity, chai is often more suitable with milk chocolate than dark; the combination creates a dreamy, ethereal effect.

1 cup cacao powder

1 cup cacao butter, liquefied

½ cup coconut oil

1½ cups liquid sweetener

¼ cup almond milk

2 tablespoons water

1 tablespoon vanilla extract

1 teaspoon cinnamon

1 teaspoon nutmeg

½ teaspoon cloves

¼ teaspoon salt

Blend all ingredients until smooth.

Prepare a 9-inch square cheesecake pan by greasing the sides with coconut oil and lining the bottom with parchment paper. Pour blended ingredients into prepared pan. Freeze for at least 1 hour to set. Fudge can be stored in the freezer or refrigerator for several weeks.

Makes approximately 3 dozen 1-inch pieces

Maca, Macadamia

If you're a fan of Lucuma like we are, try adding it to this recipe for a more Peruvian-inspired "fudge."

1 cup cacao powder

1 cup cacao butter, liquefied

½ cup coconut oil

1½ cups liquid sweetener

¼ cup almond milk

2 tablespoons maca

¼ teaspoon salt

1 tablespoon vanilla extract

1 cup macadamia nuts, chopped

Blend all ingredients except for macadamia nuts until smooth. Stir in chopped nuts.

Prepare a 9-inch square cheesecake pan by greasing the sides with coconut oil and lining the bottom with parchment paper. Pour blended ingredients into prepared pan. Freeze for at least 1 hour to set. Fudge can be stored in the freezer or refrigerator for several weeks.

Makes approximately 3 dozen 1-inch pieces

Dark Chocolate Ganache

Rich, dark, and handsome!

1½ cups cacao powder

1½ cups cacao butter, liquefied

1½ cups liquid sweetener

1 tablespoon vanilla extract

Pinch salt

Blend all ingredients until smooth.

Prepare a 9-inch square cheesecake pan by greasing the sides with coconut oil and lining the bottom with parchment paper. Pour blended ingredients into prepared pan. Freeze for at least 1 hour to set. Fudge can be stored in the freezer or refrigerator for several weeks.

Makes approximately 3 dozen 1-inch pieces

Superfood Fudge

If you're ever going on a long drive, mountain hike, or ski trip and are looking for that one bite that will give you explosive energy, here it is. Chocolate nutrition at its best.

1 cup cacao powder

1 cup cacao butter, liquefied

½ cup almond butter

1½ cups liquid sweetener

1 tablespoon vanilla extract

1 tablespoon spirulina

1 tablespoon maca

Pinch salt

½ cup goji berries, chopped

½ cup hemp seeds

¼ cup sunflower seeds, chopped

Blend all ingredients except for goji berries, hemp seeds, and sunflower seeds until smooth. Stir in goji berries, hemp seeds, and sunflower seeds.

Prepare a 9-inch square cheesecake pan by greasing the sides with coconut oil and lining the bottom with parchment paper. Pour blended ingredients into prepared pan. Freeze for at least 1 hour to set. Fudge can be stored in the freezer or refrigerator for several weeks.

Makes approximately 3 dozen 1-inch pieces

Cacao and Vanilla Bean

This is a basic go-to fudge recipe. It's ideal as a base to use when adding nuts, seeds, and other ingredients.

1 cup cacao powder

1 cup cacao butter, liquefied

½ cup coconut oil

1½ cups liquid sweetener

1 tablespoon vanilla extract

2 vanilla beans, scraped

2 tablespoons water

Pinch salt

Blend all ingredients until smooth.

Prepare a 9-inch square cheesecake pan by greasing the sides with coconut oil and lining the bottom with parchment paper. Pour blended ingredients into prepared pan. Freeze for at least 1 hour to set. Fudge can be stored in the freezer or refrigerator for several weeks.

Makes approximately 3 dozen 1-inch pieces

White Chocolate Marzipan

The use of coconut flour here is one of those raw food discoveries that happened by accident. It creates a chewy, tangy texture and flavor; along with the almond extract, it is very similar to how marzipan would be in fudge.

1 cup cashews, soaked

1 cup cacao butter, liquefied

1 cup coconut butter

1½ cups liquid sweetener

½ cup coconut flour

1 tablespoon almond extract

2 tablespoons almond milk

Pinch salt

Blend all ingredients until smooth.

Prepare a 9-inch square cheesecake pan by greasing the sides with coconut oil and lining the bottom with parchment paper. Pour blended ingredients into prepared pan. Freeze for at least 1 hour to set. Fudge can be stored in the freezer or refrigerator for several weeks.

Makes approximately 3 dozen 1-inch pieces

Almond Praline Fudge

As with many of our recipes, this one offers a great opportunity for substitution. In fact, although not as easy to find, macadamia butter is incredible as a replacement for almond.

Fudge

1 cup cacao powder

1 cup cacao butter

½ cup almond butter

1½ cups liquid sweetener

1 tablespoon vanilla extract

1 tablespoon almond extract (optional)

Pinch salt

Almond Swirl

½ cup almond butter

½ cup liquid sweetener

1 teaspoon vanilla extract

Pinch salt

Blend all ingredients for fudge until smooth. In a separate bowl, blend all ingredients for almond swirl until smooth.

Prepare a 9-inch square cheesecake pan by greasing the sides with coconut oil and lining the bottom with parchment paper. Pour blended fudge ingredients into prepared pan and refrigerate for approximately 20 minutes until slightly firm. Pour almond swirl mixture in thin lines on top of the fudge and swirl in using a chopstick or another thin utensil. Freeze for at least 1 hour to set. Fudge can be stored in the freezer or refrigerator for several weeks.

Makes approximately 3 dozen 1-inch pieces

Maple Walnut

Think of this recipe as a template for whatever sweetener/nut combination that you prefer, including pistachio-honey, macadamia–coconut nectar, almond-agave. The opportunities are quite broad.

1 cup cacao powder

1 cup cacao butter

½ cup walnut butter

1½ cups maple syrup

1 tablespoon vanilla extract

1 tablespoon walnut extract (optional)

Pinch salt

Blend all ingredients until smooth.

Prepare a 9-inch square cheesecake pan by greasing the sides with coconut oil and lining the bottom with parchment paper. Pour blended ingredients into prepared pan. Freeze for at least 1 hour to set. Fudge can be stored in the freezer or refrigerator for several weeks.

Makes approximately 3 dozen 1-inch pieces

Gianduja

Gianduja is much like a healthy fudge version of Nutella; kids (and adults) will love this.

1 cup cacao powder

1 cup cacao butter

½ cup hazelnut butter

1½ cups liquid sweetener

1 tablespoon vanilla extract

1 tablespoon hazelnut extract

Garnish
Chopped hazelnuts

Blend all ingredients until smooth.

Prepare a 9-inch square cheesecake pan by greasing the sides with coconut oil and lining the bottom with parchment paper. Pour blended ingredients into prepared pan. Garnish with chopped hazelnuts. Freeze for at least 1 hour to set. Can be stored in the freezer or refrigerator for several weeks.

Makes approximately 3 dozen 1-inch pieces

Fruit

Fruit and chocolate have a long and lovely history together and have produced some of our most memorable food experiences. On occasion, especially after a heavier meal, it is nice to enjoy chocolate that isn't quite as rich—pairing it with fruit has a lightening effect, offering a bit of freshness while still being indulgent. As you'll notice, many of our recipes use dried fruit, which is easier to work with and more stable. However, there are some special-occasion dishes that are ideal for fresh fruit as well. Of course, you can always just melt the chocolate and dip your freshest and favorite fruit right into it!

Moroccan Dates

This recipe is another example that demonstrates our affection for all things Mediterranean.

1 dozen large medjool dates, gently pitted and
    left as whole as possible

1 melted, tempered batch of Chocolate Base
    (page 11)

Stuffing

¼ cup almonds, chopped

1 teaspoon almond oil

Pinch salt

1 teaspoon cardamom

To make stuffing, toss almonds with almond oil, salt, and cardamom. Set aside.

Stuff each date with approximately 1 tablespoon of chopped almond mixture. Spear fruit with toothpicks or bamboo skewers and dip into melted chocolate. To harden, place dipped fruit on a piece of wax paper and refrigerate. Alternatively, if you do not want your dates to have a "puddle" of chocolate around them, you can stick the toothpicks or skewers holding the fruit into a block of Styrofoam in order to let the fruit drip and dry. You can also dry on a wire rack placed over a cookie sheet.

Makes 1 dozen

Chocolate-Covered Strawberries

As classic as it gets, with a twist.

2 dozen large strawberries, washed and
  thoroughly dried

1 melted, tempered batch of Chocolate Base
  (page 11)

Spear fruit with toothpicks or bamboo skewers to dip into melted chocolate. To harden, place on a piece of wax paper and refrigerate. Alternatively, if you do not want your strawberries to have a "puddle" of chocolate around them, you can stick the toothpicks or skewers holding the fruit into a block of Styrofoam in order to let the fruit drip and dry. You can also dry on a wire rack placed over a cookie sheet.

Makes 2 dozen

Coconut Haystacks

These have a similarity to macaroons, yet are a bit richer due to the cacao oil. They remain moist and delicious for quite some time. I like them kept cool.

3 cups coconut flakes

1 cup cacao powder

¼ cup cacao nibs

½ cup coconut sugar, powdered in a spice grinder

¼ cup liquid sweetener

1 tablespoon vanilla extract

⅓ cup cacao oil, melted

In a large bowl, mix all the ingredients and stir well to combine. Using a small ice cream scoop or tablespoon, spoon rounds of the dough onto a clean tray. Refrigerate to firm.

Makes approximately 2 dozen

Chocolate-Covered Cherries

Any sweeter variety of cherry would be a perfectly suitable substitute here. If you use tart cherries, you might prefer a much sweeter base recipe.

Approximately 3 dozen Bing cherries, washed and thoroughly dried

1 melted, tempered batch of Chocolate Base (page 11)

Using the stem of the cherries, dip them into the melted chocolate. To harden, place on a piece of wax paper and refrigerate. You can also dry on a wire rack placed over a cookie sheet.

Makes 3 dozen

Ginger Pineapple

The technique used to flavor and dry the pineapple works with other tropical fruit as well.

1 dozen slices pineapple, ¼-inch thick

¼ cup lemon juice

¼ cup ginger juice

1 tablespoon ginger zest

¼ cup coconut sugar, powdered in a spice grinder

1 melted, tempered batch of Chocolate Base (page 11)

To dehydrate fruit, toss pineapple in lemon and ginger juice and allow to soak for approximately 5 minutes. This will prevent the fruit from getting dark when it dehydrates and infuse a ginger flavor into the pineapple.

Pat treated fruit dry. Toss with ginger zest and coconut sugar. Lay flat on dehydrator tray. Dehydrate for 10 to 16 hours at 118 degrees F until the fruit becomes leathery, but not sticky.

Dip dehydrated fruit chips into melted chocolate, covering it approximately halfway. To harden, place on a piece of wax paper and refrigerate. Once the chocolate is firm, the fruit can be stored at room temperature.

Makes 1 dozen

Candied Apricots

These delicious snacks are similar to the fruit glacés found all over France in gourmet candy stores.

1 dozen fresh apricots, pitted and sliced in quarters

¼ cup honey

¼ cup water

1 tablespoon vanilla extract

Pinch salt

1 melted, tempered batch of Chocolate Base (page 11)

Toss apricot quarters with honey, water, vanilla, and salt. Dehydrate at 118 degrees F for 24 hours until the apricots become chewy and "candy-like." Drizzle candied apricots with melted chocolate. Place in refrigerator to firm.

Makes approximately 4 dozen

Chocolate-Covered Turkish Figs

Figs are so good on their own when fresh and ripe, it's hard to imagine them needing anything more. However, the chocolate does give them a texture and flavor complexity, and adds a hint of elegance.

2 dozen large Turkish figs*

1 melted, tempered batch of Chocolate Base (page 11)

Spear fruit with toothpicks or bamboo skewers to dip into chocolate. To harden, place on a piece of wax paper and refrigerate. Alternatively, if you do not want your figs to have a "puddle" of chocolate around them, you can stick the toothpicks or skewers holding the fruit into a block of Styrofoam in order to let the fruit drip and dry. You can also dry on a wire rack placed over a cookie sheet.

* You can use fresh or dried figs, for two completely different dishes.

Makes 2 dozen

Chocolate Fruit Chips

My favorite is banana, but many different kinds of fruit work in this recipe. Try apples, pears, or strawberries. They work the best because they become the most crisp. The higher the sugar content in the fruit, the longer it will take to dehydrate and the less crisp the chips will be.

4 cups fruit of your choice, ¼-inch-thick slices

½ cup lemon juice

1 melted, tempered batch of Chocolate Base (page 11)

To dehydrate fruit, toss in lemon juice and allow to soak for approximately 5 minutes. This will prevent the fruit from getting dark when it dehydrates. Pat treated fruit dry. Lay flat on dehydrator tray. Dehydrate for 10 to 16 hours at 118 degrees F until the fruit becomes crisp.

Dip fruit chips into melted chocolate, covering approximately halfway. To harden, place on a piece of wax paper and refrigerate. Once the chocolate is firm, the fruit can be stored at room temperature.

Makes 4 cups

Chocolate-Banana Popsicle

Quick and easy and kids will love them!

1 melted, tempered batch of Chocolate Base (page 11)

6 medium-sized bananas, peeled

6 Popsicle sticks

1 cup chopped nuts of your choice or 1 cup cacao nibs (optional)

Slide one Popsicle stick into the end of each banana. Freeze bananas.

Remove bananas from freezer and prepare to dip them in chocolate. Chocolate will harden quickly once you dip the bananas so it is essential that you do this quickly. It is best to put the chocolate in a wide bowl or baking dish so that you can cover the most surface area of the banana at one time. Dip each banana in chocolate. Sprinkle with nuts or cacao nibs if you choose. Store in freezer.

Makes 6

Chocolate Papaya

Some recipes evolve from snacks when there is little else to eat—this is one.

1 dozen unsulfured dried papaya spears

1 melted, tempered batch of Chocolate Base (page 11)

Dip fruit into chocolate, coating each piece approximately halfway. To harden, place on a piece of wax paper and refrigerate. Once the chocolate is firm, the fruit can be stored at room temperature.

Makes 1 dozen

Le Goûter

If only airports, train stations, and sports arenas offered these snacks, as opposed to what are now traditional fast-food options, we would be a lot better off. Whereas chocolate is predominately known for its status as the world's best sweet, it also happens to do very well in a supporting healthy role. These recipes represent some of our favorite snacks that, while not dominated by chocolate, are certainly enlivened by it.

Buckwheat Nib Crispies

Take care to properly rinse and drain the buckwheat—otherwise, this snack will have a bit of a dusty character to it.

2 cups buckwheat groats, soaked for at least 1 hour

½ cup coconut sugar, powdered in a spice grinder

¼ cup water

1 tablespoon vanilla extract

½ cup cacao nibs

2 teaspoons salt

Rinse and drain buckwheat. In a food processor, add the buckwheat and all remaining ingredients. Pulse until thoroughly combined, but still slightly chunky. Spread on Teflex-lined dehydrator trays, approximately ⅛-inch thick. Dehydrate at 118 degrees F for 8 to 12 hours until the top is completely dry and you can easily remove from Teflex. Turn pieces over and continue to dehydrate for at least 2 more hours, or until completely dry. Once dry, break into pieces and store in an airtight container.

Serves 4 to 6

Chocolate-Covered Pecans

Pecans are the most buttery of all nuts, a highlight that makes this simple treat a decadent one.

1 melted, tempered batch of Chocolate Base (page 11)

2 cups pecan halves

Dip each pecan half in melted chocolate until halfway coated. Place on a tray lined with wax paper. Refrigerate to allow chocolate to set.

Makes 2 cups

Superfood Crunch Mix

A pop culture assembly of today's rock-star superfoods.

1¼ cups cacao beans

1 cup pistachios

¼ cup whole cashews

½ cup goji berries

½ cup Incan golden berries

½ cup coconut flakes

1 teaspoon Himalayan salt

Toss all ingredients together to mix.

Makes approximately 4 cups

Macadamia Brittle

We're huge fans of smoked salt these days. It not only has an incredible aroma, but also offers a woodsy, earthy depth to recipes.

1½ cups macadamia nuts, chopped

1 tablespoon smoked salt

1 melted, tempered batch of Chocolate Base
    (page 11)

Stir macadamia nuts and salt into melted chocolate. Line a cookie sheet with wax paper and spread mixture evenly over it. Allow to set in refrigerator for at least 10 minutes or until chocolate is hard.

To serve, simply break into pieces the size of your choice.

Makes approximately 4 cups

Chunky Monkey Granola

Raw granola is a great snack, excellent as a breakfast cereal with almond milk, or even to top a sundae or ice cream.

2 ripe bananas

½ cup dates, pitted

¼ cup water

¼ cup cacao powder

1 tablespoon vanilla extract

2 teaspoons cinnamon

½ teaspoon nutmeg

2 teaspoons salt

1 cup buckwheat, soaked at least 1 hour and drained

1 cup almonds, coarsely chopped

1 cup macadamia nuts, coarsely chopped

1 cup pecans, coarsely chopped

¼ cup cacao nibs

1½ cups coconut flakes

Blend bananas, dates, water, cacao powder, vanilla, spices, and salt until completely smooth to make a banana paste. In a mixing bowl, toss remaining ingredients with banana paste. Spread on dehydrator trays and dehydrate at 118 degrees F for approximately 24 hours, until crisp.

Break up into pieces the size you desire.

Makes approximately 6 cups

Candied Almond Clusters

Although almonds are our nut of choice for the clusters, pecans, Brazil nuts, or walnuts would work well also.

4 cups almonds, soaked, rinsed, and drained

½ cup coconut sugar, powdered in a spice grinder

½ cup cacao powder

1 tablespoon vanilla extract

2 teaspoons sea salt

Drain the almonds well and place them in a large bowl with remaining ingredients; toss well to coat. Pour the nuts onto dehydrator sheets and dehydrate at 118 degrees F for 6 to 8 hours, until crisp.

Makes 4 cups

Ginger Cacao Cashews

These would also be great in a savory dish, such as an arugula salad with lemon.

4 cups whole cashews, soaked, rinsed, and drained

½ cup coconut sugar, powdered in a spice grinder

½ cup cacao powder

2 tablespoons ginger zest

1 tablespoon vanilla extract

2 teaspoons sea salt

Drain the cashews well and place them in a large bowl with remaining ingredients; toss well to coat. Pour the nuts onto dehydrator sheets and dehydrate at 118 degrees F for 6 to 8 hours, until crisp.

Makes 4 cups

Cacao Energy Bites

Similar to a granola bar, these are great when you're
on the go.

4 cups almonds, ground to a fine powder in a
food processor

1½ cups sunflower seeds

1½ cups pumpkin seeds

1 cup hemp seeds

½ cup golden flax seeds, soaked for 2 hours
and drained

½ cup cacao nibs

1 cup dried berries (Incan golden berries, goji
berries, or mulberries)

1¼ cups liquid sweetener

¼ cup maca

2 tablespoons spirulina

1 tablespoon vanilla extract

2 teaspoons salt

Mix all ingredients in a large bowl until well combined. Spread evenly on a lined
dehydrator tray. Dehydrate at 118 degrees F for 10 to 12 hours until dry, but still
chewy. Slice into 2-inch squares.

Makes about 4 dozen

Cacao Crunch Mix

For some, whole cacao beans are a bit pungent. Feel free to chop them or reduce the quantity in this recipe if you prefer.

1 cup cacao beans

¼ cacao nibs

½ cup almonds

½ cup walnuts

½ cup coconut flakes

1 tablespoon coconut oil

1 tablespoon cacao powder

1 tablespoon grated orange peel

Pinch salt

Toss all ingredients in a large mixing bowl.

Makes approximately 4 cups

Sweet and Salty

If you have access to the plump golden Hunza raisins, they're highly recommended here!

½ cup dates, pitted and finely chopped

¼ cup raisins (Hunza raisins preferred)

½ cup cacao nibs

½ cup pumpkin seeds

½ cup sunflower seeds

2 tablespoons olive oil

2 teaspoons coarse salt

Toss all ingredients in a large mixing bowl until well combined.

Makes approximately 4 cups

Smoothies and Drinks

Smoothies are still the go-to food for quick nutrition and flavor. These days, with the abundance of high-quality chocolate products on the market, there are more options than ever for enlivening your beverage with cacao. As this is a chocolate book, and therefore all about decadence, many of our smoothie recipes could as easily be enjoyed as dessert, not just breakfast.

Midnight Chocolate

We love green smoothies! If you have high-quality fresh kale or spinach, it would make an excellent substitute for the spirulina. Or use both for an extra green drink.

1¼ cups blueberries, frozen

½ cup fresh young coconut

1¼ cups coconut water

1 tablespoon cacao butter

¼ cup cacao powder

¼ cup cacao nibs

1 tablespoon liquid sweetener

1 teaspoon vanilla extract

1 tablespoon spirulina (optional)

Pinch sea salt

Blend all ingredients in a high-speed blender until smooth.

Makes 1 to 2 servings

Amaretto Buttercup

Some are not fans of the grainy texture that nibs provide when blended in a drink. We happen to prefer the crunch, but you can always use cacao powder instead of nibs for a smooth drink.

1½ cups cherries, frozen

2 tablespoons almond butter

1¼ cups almond milk

1 tablespoon coconut butter

¼ cup cacao nibs

1 tablespoon liquid sweetener (or 1 large date)

1 teaspoon vanilla extract

½ teaspoon amaretto extract (optional)

Pinch sea salt

Blend all ingredients in a high-speed blender until smooth.

Makes 1 to 2 servings

Hot Chocolate

You don't normally associate the word *hot* with raw food, but this drink can get surprisingly warm in the blender. It's a delicious addition to a cold day!

2 cups warm water

4 tablespoons liquid sweetener

¼ cup cacao powder

1½ tablespoons coconut butter

1 teaspoon vanilla

Pinch of salt

¼ cup hemp seeds (optional)

Blend all ingredients until smooth and warm, approximately one full minute. For an extra filling, nutritious, and creamy drink, add hemp seeds.

Makes 2 to 4 servings

Frappuccino

This will surely offer far more nutrition, not to mention flavor and energy, than your local Starbucks version.

1½ cups fresh young coconut

½ cup ice

1¼ cups coffee, preferably cold pressed

1 tablespoon cacao butter, liquefied

1 tablespoon coconut butter

½ cup cacao powder

2 tablespoons liquid sweetener

1 teaspoon vanilla extract

Pinch sea salt

Blend all ingredients in a high-speed blender until smooth.

Makes 1 to 2 servings

Mint Chocolate Chip

Bananas are so helpful when kept frozen. You can use them in smoothies or desserts or even to make a plain banana ice cream (you can make ice cream in many juicers with the flat side of the blade facing out). Keep them until very ripe, then peel, chop, and freeze in ziplock bags.

1¼ cups banana chunks, frozen

½ cup fresh young coconut

1¼ cups coconut water

1 tablespoon cacao butter

1 teaspoon vanilla extract

1 teaspoon peppermint extract

1 tablespoon liquid sweetener

4 to 5 fresh mint leaves

1 tablespoon spirulina (optional)

Pinch sea salt

Blend all ingredients in a high-speed blender until smooth.

Makes 1 to 2 servings

Maple Chocolate Milk

Adding maple syrup to this chocolate milk makes the flavor even more rich and decadent.

2 cups almond milk (or nut milk of choice)

4 tablespoons maple syrup

¼ cup cacao powder

1½ tablespoons coconut butter

1 teaspoon vanilla extract

Pinch salt

Garnish

Maple sugar

Cacao powder

Blend all ingredients until smooth. This drink can be served warm or cold. Garnish with maple sugar and cacao powder.

Makes 2 to 4 servings

Xocolat

There is so much good about this drink—you could easily live on it for a few days if ever stranded on a remote island with nothing else.

1¼ cups pineapple chunks, frozen

½ cup fresh young coconut

1¼ cups coconut water

1 tablespoon cacao butter

¼ cup cacao powder

1 Thai chile, seeds removed

1-inch chunk ginger

1 teaspoon vanilla extract

¼ teaspoon cinnamon

¼ teaspoon cayenne

Pinch sea salt

Blend all ingredients in a high-speed blender until smooth.

Makes 1 to 2 servings

Banana Split

Admittedly, there is a fair amount of work involved if you follow this recipe in its entirety. But you—and especially your kids—will love it.

Smoothie Base

1¼ cups banana chunks, frozen

½ cup fresh young coconut

1¼ cups coconut water

1 tablespoon cacao butter

1 tablespoon liquid sweetener

Pinch sea salt

2 tablespoons Cacao Swirl

Cacao Swirl

1½ cups cacao nibs

1¼ cups liquid sweetener

½ cup coconut oil

2 tablespoons chopped Chocolate-Covered
   Pecans (page 105)

To make cacao swirl, blend all ingredients in a high-speed blender until smooth.

Blend all ingredients for smoothie base in a high-speed blender until smooth. Stir in cacao swirl and chopped pecans.

Makes 1 to 2 servings

Tropical Coconut, Cacao Bean

You may notice that our smoothies rarely have ice. We believe in creating as much flavor intensity as possible, and ice, although cooling, dilutes taste. The frozen fruit in our recipes replaces the need for ice and allows for a very creamy texture when blending.

1 cup pineapple chunks, frozen

¼ cup fresh young Thai coconut

½ cup coconut flakes (or mature coconut meat)

1¼ cups coconut water

1 tablespoon coconut butter

1 tablespoon liquid sweetener

1 teaspoon vanilla extract

Pinch sea salt

¼ cup cacao nibs

Blend all ingredients except cacao nibs in a high-speed blender until smooth. Blend in nibs until combined, but still slightly chunky.

Makes 1 to 2 servings

Malted Maca Milkshake

Maca, the wonder root from Peru, is noted for its energy-producing properties. It has an interesting, earthy character, which when combined with sweetness and especially with chocolate, creates a natural malted effect.

1¼ cups banana chunks, frozen

½ cup fresh young coconut

1¼ cups coconut water

1 tablespoon cacao butter

¼ cup cacao powder

2 tablespoons maca

1 tablespoon liquid sweetener

1 teaspoon vanilla extract

Pinch sea salt

Blend all ingredients in a high-speed blender until smooth.

Makes 1 to 2 servings

Buttercups

We all love things in nice little packages, especially when the package itself is made from chocolate! It's easy to understand the fascination with peanut butter cups, although the widely available commercial brands could improve a great deal in terms of the quality of ingredients they use. The recipes we offer in this chapter take a lot of liberty from the original concept, but remain true to the spirit of buttercups. They are fun to eat and pretty to look at. In concept, they've always been great—we've just taken a bit of liberty with the flavors.

Cookies and Cream

For reformed junk food aficionados, think of this as a peanut butter cup base, filled with frozen Oreo ice cream. You get the idea!

1 melted, tempered batch of Chocolate Base (page 11)

Filling

1½ cups cashews

½ cup liquid sweetener

½ cup water

½ cup fresh young coconut

⅓ cup coconut oil, melted

⅓ cup coconut butter

1 tablespoon vanilla extract

Pinch salt

½ cup cacao nibs

Filling
Blend all ingredients except cacao nibs until smooth. Stir in nibs.

Assembly
Prepare a muffin pan with paper liners. You can use a 24-cup mini muffin pan or a standard 12-cup size. The smaller size is preferable because the chocolates are very dense and rich.

This is a three-step process that requires firming each layer before you add the next. To begin, fill cups one-fourth of the way full with melted chocolate and place in the refrigerator to firm. Once the bottom chocolate layer is firm, pour in filling approximately two-thirds of the way. Place pan in freezer for filling to firm for approximately 1 hour. Once filling is firm, pour in remaining chocolate to fill. Place in the refrigerator or freezer to firm for at least 30 minutes before serving.

Makes 24 mini or 12 large buttercups

Blueberry Bliss

We write and produce all of our books on the coast of Maine, the best place in the world for wild blueberries. These delicious berries make an appearance whenever we write and cook.

1 melted, tempered batch of Chocolate Base
(page 11)

Filling

1½ cups cashews

½ cup liquid sweetener

½ cup water

½ cup fresh young coconut

⅓ cup coconut oil, melted

⅓ cup coconut butter

¼ cup frozen blueberries

1 tablespoon maqui powder (optional to make a deeper color)

1 tablespoon vanilla extract

Pinch salt

Filling
Blend all ingredients until smooth.

Assembly
Prepare a muffin pan with paper liners. You can use a 24-cup mini muffin pan or a standard 12-cup size. The smaller size is preferable because the chocolates are very dense and rich.

This is a three-step process that requires firming each layer before you add the next. To begin, fill cups one-fourth of the way full with melted chocolate and place in the refrigerator to firm. Once the bottom chocolate layer is firm, pour in filling approximately two-thirds of the way. Place pan in freezer for filling to firm for approximately 1 hour. Once filling is firm, pour in remaining chocolate to fill. Place in the refrigerator or freezer to firm for at least 30 minutes before serving.

Makes 24 mini or 12 large buttercups

Tiramisu

I still recall my first day at work in a professional kitchen (which happened to be Sicilian). My station was right next to the pastry cooler where Beth, the pastry chef, stored her delicious tiramisu. I've loved it ever since.

1 melted, tempered batch of Chocolate Base
(page 11)

Filling

1½ cups cashews

½ cup liquid sweetener

½ cup cold-pressed coffee

½ cup fresh young coconut

⅓ cup coconut oil

⅓ cup coconut butter

1 tablespoon finely ground coffee beans

1 tablespoon vanilla extract

Pinch salt

Filling
Blend all ingredients until smooth.

Assembly
Prepare a muffin pan with paper liners. You can use a 24-cup mini muffin pan or a standard 12-cup size. The smaller size is preferable because the chocolates are very dense and rich.

This is a three-step process that requires firming each layer before you add the next. To begin, fill cups one-fourth of the way full with melted chocolate and place in the refrigerator to firm. Once the bottom chocolate layer is firm, pour in filling approximately two-thirds of the way. Place pan in freezer for filling to firm for approximately 1 hour. Once filling is firm, pour in remaining chocolate to fill. Place in the refrigerator or freezer to firm for at least 30 minutes before serving.

Makes 24 mini or 12 large buttercups

Black Forest

The Black Forest cake is originally named for the use of a cherry liqueur from that region of Germany. Feel free to use the liqueur, although the cherries and chocolate are more than capable on their own.

1 melted, tempered batch of Chocolate Base (page 11)

Filling

1 cup cashews

½ cup almond butter

½ cup liquid sweetener

½ cup water

½ cup black cherries, frozen

2 tablespoons Kirschwasser (optional)

½ cup fresh young coconut

⅓ cup coconut oil

⅓ cup coconut butter

1 tablespoon vanilla extract

1 tablespoon beet juice (optional to make a deeper color)

1 teaspoon amaretto extract

Pinch salt

Filling
Blend all ingredients until smooth.

Assembly
Prepare a muffin pan with paper liners. You can use a 24-cup mini muffin pan or a standard 12-cup size. The smaller size is preferable because the chocolates are very dense and rich.

This is a three-step process that requires firming each layer before you add the next. To begin, fill cups one-fourth of the way full with melted chocolate and place in the refrigerator to firm. Once the bottom chocolate layer is firm, pour in filling approximately two-thirds of the way. Place pan in freezer for filling to firm for approximately 1 hour. Once filling is firm, pour in remaining chocolate to fill. Place in the refrigerator or freezer to firm for at least 30 minutes before serving.

Makes 24 mini or 12 large buttercups

Blood Orange

Blood oranges are seasonal, so we have allowed a regular orange (of any variety) to act as a substitute.

1 melted, tempered batch of Chocolate Base (page 11)

Filling

1½ cups cashews

½ cup liquid sweetener

½ cup freshly squeezed blood orange juice*

½ cup fresh young coconut

¼ cup blood orange pulp**
  (seeds and membranes removed)

⅓ cup coconut oil

⅓ cup coconut butter

1 tablespoon vanilla extract

Pinch salt

* Regular orange juice may be substituted if blood oranges are not in season.
** Regular orange pulp may be substituted.

Filling
Blend all ingredients until smooth.

Assembly
Prepare a muffin pan with paper liners. You can use a 24-cup mini muffin pan or a standard 12-cup size. The smaller size is preferable because the chocolates are very dense and rich.

This is a three-step process that requires firming each layer before you add the next. To begin, fill cups one-fourth of the way full with melted chocolate and place in the refrigerator to firm. Once the bottom chocolate layer is firm, pour in filling approximately two-thirds of the way. Place pan in freezer for filling to firm for approximately 1 hour. Once filling is firm, pour in remaining chocolate to fill. Place in the refrigerator or freezer to firm for at least 30 minutes before serving.

Makes 24 mini or 12 large buttercups

Strawberry

The technique here is suitable for any other berry, or a combination of them, as well. Experiment.

1 melted, tempered batch of Chocolate Base (page 11)

Filling

1½ cups cashews

½ cup liquid sweetener

½ cup water

½ cup strawberries, frozen

½ cup fresh young coconut

⅓ cup coconut oil

⅓ cup coconut butter

1 tablespoon vanilla extract

Pinch salt

Filling
Blend all ingredients until smooth.

Assembly
Prepare a muffin pan with paper liners. You can use a 24-cup mini muffin pan or a standard 12-cup size. The smaller size is preferable because the chocolates are very dense and rich.

This is a three-step process that requires firming each layer before you add the next. To begin, fill cups one-fourth of the way full with melted chocolate and place in the refrigerator to firm. Once the bottom chocolate layer is firm, pour in filling approximately two-thirds of the way. Place pan in freezer for filling to firm for approximately 1 hour. Once filling is firm, pour in remaining chocolate to fill. Place in the refrigerator or freezer to firm for at least 30 minutes before serving.

Makes 24 mini or 12 large buttercups

Lemon Zest

As with many citrus recipes, you should feel free to experiment with other zests, such as red grapefruit, orange, and even lime.

1 melted, tempered batch of Chocolate Base (page 11)

Filling

1½ cups cashews

½ cup liquid sweetener

¼ cup water

¼ cup freshly squeezed lemon juice

½ cup young Thai coconut meat

⅓ cup coconut oil, melted

⅓ cup coconut butter, liquefied

2 tablespoons lemon zest

1 tablespoon vanilla extract

Pinch salt

Filling
Blend all ingredients until smooth.

Assembly
Prepare a muffin pan with paper liners. You can use a 24-cup mini muffin pan or a standard 12-cup size. The smaller size is preferable because the chocolates are very dense and rich.

This is a three-step process that requires firming each layer before you add the next. To begin, fill cups one-fourth of the way full with melted chocolate and place in the refrigerator to firm. Once the bottom chocolate layer is firm, pour in filling approximately two-thirds of the way. Place pan in freezer for filling to firm for approximately 1 hour. Once filling is firm, pour in remaining chocolate to fill. Place in the refrigerator or freezer to firm for at least 30 minutes before serving.

Makes 24 mini or 12 large buttercups

German Chocolate

I recall that my favorite birthday cake used to be German chocolate, and we included a raw recipe for it in *Everyday Raw Desserts.* While that recipe had no chocolate at all, just cacao powder, we wanted to include it again here, as German chocolate is a classic favorite and this is one of my favorite dessert combinations.

1 melted, tempered batch of Chocolate Base (page 11)

Filling

1 cup cashews

½ cup pecan butter

¾ cup liquid sweetener

¼ cup water

¼ cup cacao powder

½ cup fresh young coconut

⅓ cup coconut oil, melted

⅓ cup coconut butter

1 tablespoon vanilla extract

Pinch salt

¼ cup coconut flakes

¼ cup pecans, chopped

Filling

Blend all ingredients except coconut flakes and chopped pecans until smooth. Stir in coconut flakes and pecans.

Assembly

Prepare a muffin pan with paper liners. You can use a 24-cup mini muffin pan or a standard 12-cup size. The smaller size is preferable because the chocolates are very dense and rich.

This is a three-step process that requires firming each layer before you add the next. To begin, fill cups one-fourth of the way full with melted chocolate and place in the refrigerator to firm. Once the bottom chocolate layer is firm, pour in filling approximately two-thirds of the way. Place pan in freezer for filling to firm for approximately 1 hour. Once filling is firm, pour in remaining chocolate to fill. Place in the refrigerator or freezer to firm for at least 30 minutes before serving.

Makes 24 mini or 12 large buttercups

Coconut Dream

Extracts and, occasionally, essential oils provide wonderful clarity of flavor, especially in dishes that are more one-dimensional to start with. If you can find them, we highly recommend their inclusion.

1 melted, tempered batch of Chocolate
   Base (page 11)

Filling

1½ cups cashews

½ cup liquid sweetener

½ cup water

¾ cup fresh young coconut

⅓ cup coconut oil

⅓ cup coconut butter

1 tablespoon vanilla extract

1 teaspoon organic coconut extract (optional)

Pinch salt

Filling

Blend all ingredients until smooth.

Assembly

Prepare a muffin pan with paper liners. You can use a 24-cup mini muffin pan or a standard 12-cup size. The smaller size is preferable because the chocolates are very dense and rich.

This is a three-step process that requires firming each layer before you add the next. To begin, fill cups one-fourth of the way full with melted chocolate and place in the refrigerator to firm. Once the bottom chocolate layer is firm, pour in filling approximately two-thirds of the way. Place pan in freezer for filling to firm for approximately 1 hour. Once filling is firm, pour in remaining chocolate to fill. Place in the refrigerator or freezer to firm for at least 30 minutes before serving.

Makes 24 mini or 12 large buttercups

Chocolate Soufflé

While coconut meat is rich, it is also high in water content and when blended in a filling, or an ice cream, it lends a fluffiness and lightness to the dish—thus the "soufflé" label for this recipe.

1 melted, tempered batch of Chocolate
   Base (page 11)

Filling

1½ cups cashews

½ cup cacao powder

½ cup liquid sweetener

½ cup water

¾ cup fresh young coconut

⅓ cup coconut oil

½ cup coconut butter

1 tablespoon vanilla extract

Pinch salt

Filling

Blend all ingredients until smooth.

Assembly

Prepare a muffin pan with paper liners. You can use a 24-cup mini muffin pan or a standard 12-cup size. The smaller size is preferable because the chocolates are very dense and rich.

This is a three-step process that requires firming each layer before you add the next. To begin, fill cups one-fourth of the way full with melted chocolate and place in the refrigerator to firm. Once the bottom chocolate layer is firm, pour in filling approximately two-thirds of the way. Place pan in freezer for filling to firm for approximately 1 hour. Once filling is firm, pour in remaining chocolate to fill. Place in the refrigerator or freezer to firm for at least 30 minutes before serving.

Makes 24 mini or 12 large buttercups

Index

Metric Conversion Chart

Volume Measurements		Weight Measurements		Temperature Conversion	
U.S.	**Metric**	**U.S.**	**Metric**	**Fahrenheit**	**Celsius**
1 teaspoon	5 ml	½ ounce	15 g	250	120
1 tablespoon	15 ml	1 ounce	30 g	300	150
¼ cup	60 ml	3 ounces	90 g	325	160
⅓ cup	75 ml	4 ounces	115 g	350	180
½ cup	125 ml	8 ounces	225 g	375	190
⅔ cup	150 ml	12 ounces	350 g	400	200
¾ cup	175 ml	1 pound	450 g	425	220
1 cup	250 ml	2¼ pounds	1 kg	450	230